P9-DGX-192

George Washington

by Wil Mara

Content Consultant

Nanci R. Vargus, Ed.D.
Professor Emeritus, University of Indianapolis

Reading Consultant

Jeanne Clidas, Ph.D.

Children's Press®
An Imprint of Scholastic Inc.
New York Toronto London Auckland Sydney
Mexico City New Delhi Hong Kong
Danbury, Connecticut

Cataloging-in-Publication Data is available from the Library of Congress

ISBN 978-0-531-24736-5 (lib. bdg.)
ISBN 978-0-531-24702-0 (pbk.)

No part of this publication may be reproduced in whole or in part, or stored in a retrieval system, or transmitted in any form or by any means, electronic, mechanical, photocopying, recording, or otherwise, without written permission of the publisher. For information regarding permission, write to Scholastic Inc., Attention: Permissions Department, 557 Broadway, New York, NY 10012.

Produced by Spooky Cheetah Press
Poem by Jodie Shepherd

© 2013 by Scholastic Inc.

All rights reserved. Published in 2013 by Children's Press, an imprint of Scholastic Inc.

Printed in China 62

SCHOLASTIC, CHILDREN'S PRESS, ROOKIE BIOGRAPHIES®, and associated logos are trademarks and/or registered trademarks of Scholastic Inc.

1 2 3 4 5 6 7 8 9 10 R 22 21 20 19 18 17 16 15 14 13

Photographs © 2013: Alamy Images: 3 top right (Anne Rippy), 28 (Jack Sullivan), 3 bottom, 30 right (jvphoto); AP Images: 24 top (Heritage Auctions), 11, 12, 15, 31 center top, 31 bottom (North Wind Picture Archives); Bridgeman Art Library/Private Collection/Peter Newark American Pictures: 19; Library of Congress/Currier & Ives: 8, 30 left; Shutterstock, Inc.: 24 bottom left (.AGA.), 27 (fstockfoto), 24 bottom right (mikeledray), 3 top left (Rudy Balasko); Superstock, Inc.: cover (Emanuel Gottlieb Leutze), 16 (Junius Brutus Stearns), 4, 31 center bottom (Rembrandt Peale), 23 (Steve Vidler); The Granger Collection/Howard Chandler Christy: 20.

Maps by XNR Productions, Inc.

Table of Contents

Meet George Washington **5**
The Fight for Freedom **10**
A New Start **17**
President Washington **21**
Timeline **28**
A Poem about George Washington **30**
You Can Be a Leader **30**
Glossary 31
Index 32
Facts for Now 32
About the Author 32

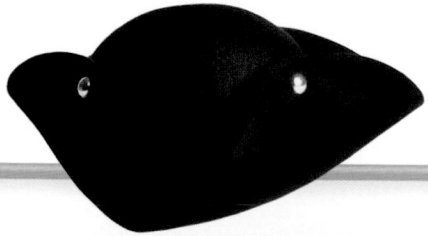

Meet George Washington

George Washington helped the United States become a free country. He was also the nation's first **President**.

Washington is known as the "Father of Our Country."

George Washington was born in Virginia.

George was born in Virginia on February 22, 1732. His family had a large farm. George was a solider when he was young. A soldier is someone who fights for his or her country.

FAST FACT!

When he was 26 years old, George married Martha Custis.

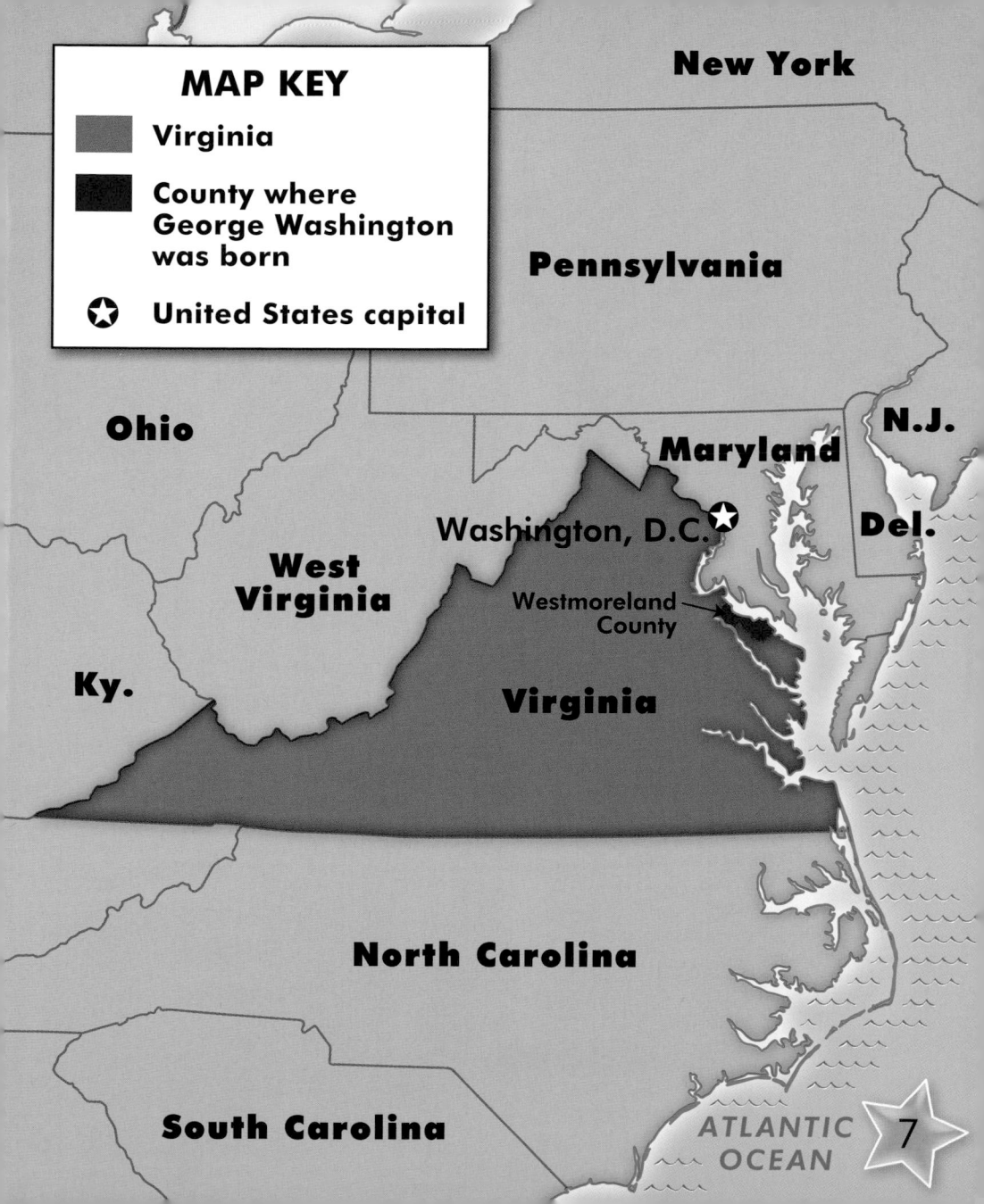
MAP KEY
Virginia
County where George Washington was born
United States capital
New York
Pennsylvania
Ohio
Maryland
N.J.
Del.
Washington, D.C.
West Virginia
Westmoreland County
Ky.
Virginia
North Carolina
South Carolina
ATLANTIC OCEAN

At first, America was an English **colony**. It was ruled by the king of England. Many Americans did not like this. They wanted America to be a free country. George was one of these people.

Washington was chosen to lead American troops in a war against England.

The Fight for Freedom

In 1775, the American colonies went to **war** with England. George was in charge of the American army. He was a **general**.

Washington was one of America's best soldiers.

The English army had more soldiers than the American army. Their soldiers had been in many wars before. They were sure they would win this one.

The English soldiers wore red coats. The Americans wore blue.

The leader of England's army told Washington: We give up.

Most of the Americans had never fought in a war. But George was a good general. His soldiers fought hard for him. America won the war in 1781. The country was free at last!

FAST FACT!

George had fake teeth. Many people think they were made of wood. But they were actually made of ivory.

A New Start

America had to start its own government. A government is a group of people that runs a country.

America's leaders met to talk about the new government.

George was a hero in America. Many people wanted him to be the country's first President. He was elected in 1789.

After the war, crowds of people came out to watch General Washington parade through the streets.

President Washington

President George Washington worked with other leaders to write laws for the new nation. A law is a rule that people have to follow.

America's leaders worked together to make laws for the country.

President Washington put together the first Supreme Court. The Court is made up of people who study and explain the laws of the nation.

This is a photo of the Supreme Court building today.

NE FIRST ST

Front and back of the first American money

Front and back of an American dollar from 2013

Before the war, Americans used English money. President Washington wanted America to have its own money. The leaders of the country worked together to create the new money.

The President got to decide where the nation's capital would be. That is where the government is located. He picked the place that is known today as Washington, D.C.

FAST FACT!

Washington never lived in Washington, D.C. When he was President, New York City and, later, Philadelphia were the nation's capitals.

Washington
Monument

Timeline of George Washington's Life

1732
born on February 22

1775–1781
leads American troops in war against England

Today people can visit George Washington's house.

People wanted Washington to continue as President for many years. But he wanted to go home to his farm and his family. In 1797, he went back to Virginia. He died there two years later.

1789
becomes America's first President

1797
leaves the presidency to go back to Virginia

1799
dies on December 14

A Poem About George Washington

He led our fight for freedom,
then led the U.S.A.
It's thanks to brave George Washington
we can live free today.

You Can Be a Leader

- You can set a good example for others by always trying to do what you think is right.
- Do not be afraid to stand up for what you believe in—even if others say you are wrong.

Glossary

colony (KOL-uh-nee): a place that is settled by people from another country

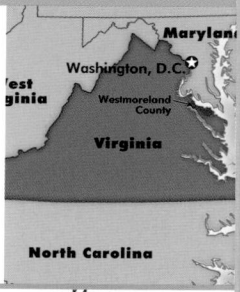

general (JEN-ur-all): a solider of very high rank who leads other soldiers

president (PREZ-uh-duhnt): the elected leader of a country

war (wor): a fight between two or more groups of people

Index

capital 26
England 9, 10
family 6, 29
freedom 5, 9, 14
government 17, 26
laws 21, 22
money 24, 25
president 5, 18, 21, 22, 25, 26, 29
soldier 6, 13, 14
Supreme Court 22
war 10, 13, 14, 25

Facts for Now

Visit this Scholastic Web site for more information on George Washington:
www.factsfornow.scholastic.com
Enter the keywords **George Washington**

About the Author

Wil Mara is the award-winning author of more than 140 books, many of which are educational titles for children.